Pets, Animals & Creatures

Designed and illustrated by Jane Phillips, Kathy Kifer and Marina Krasnik

Published by
Garlic Press
605 Powers St.
Eugene, OR 97402

Soft Cover
ISBN 0-931993-89-X
Order No. GP-089

Hard Cover
ISBN 1-930820-39-9
Order No. GP-139
Printed in China

www.garlicpress.com

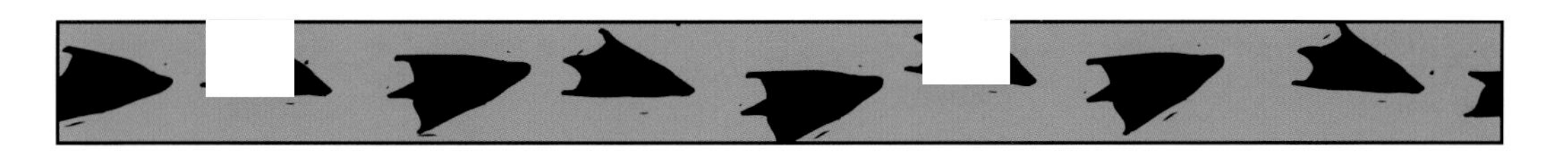

Pets, Animals & Creatures is part of the Beginning Sign Language Series. The pets, animals, and creatures pictured are accompanied by their signs. While more than one sign may exist for a particular pet, animal, or creature, we have tried to use the most graphic representation or the most widely used sign to accompany each picture.

The book is organized into color-coded sections as follows:

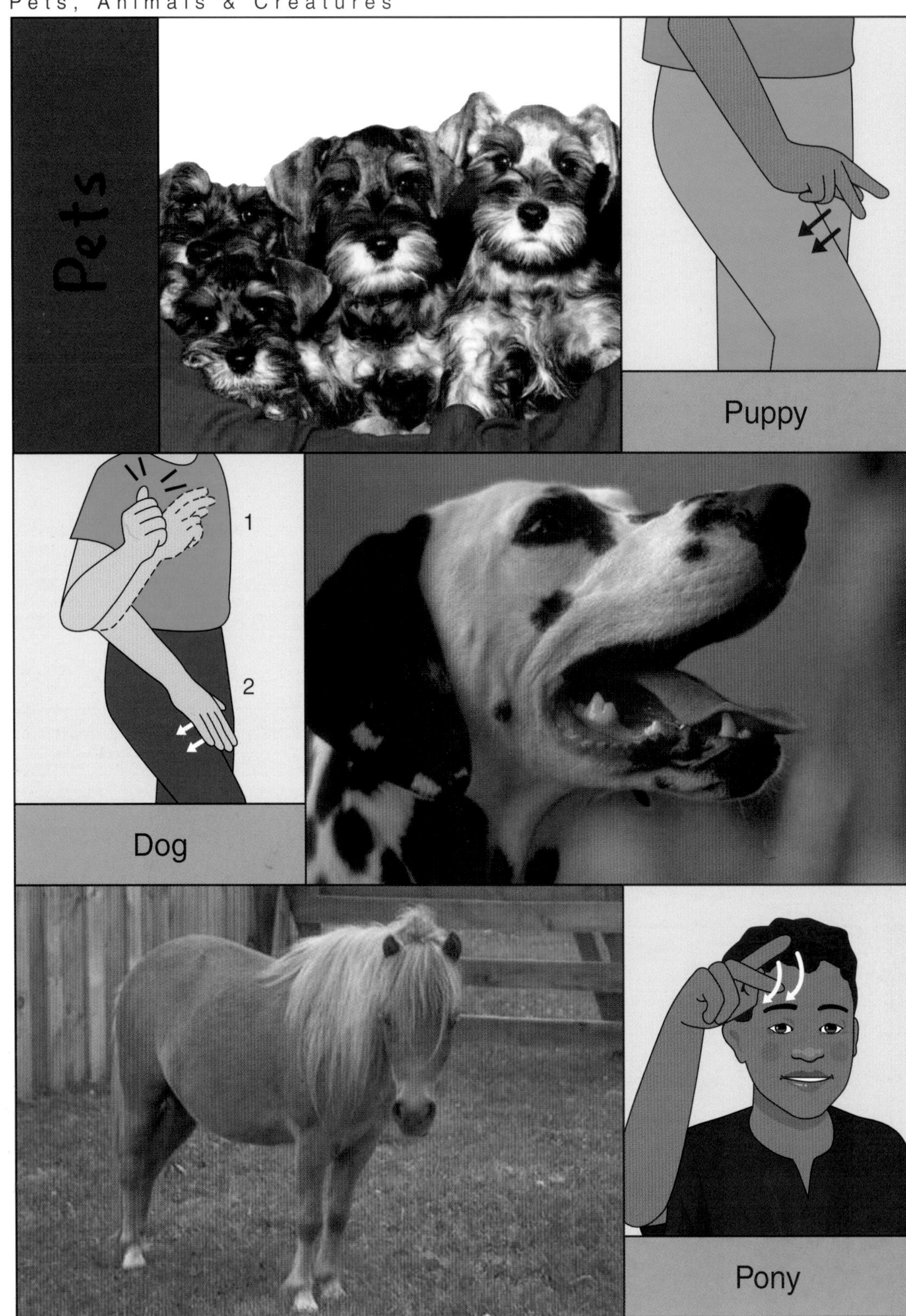

Puppy

Dog

Pony

Pets
Cat
Kitten
Fish

Pets
Mouse
Bunny
1
2
Canary

Pets
Parrot
Pigeon
Turtle

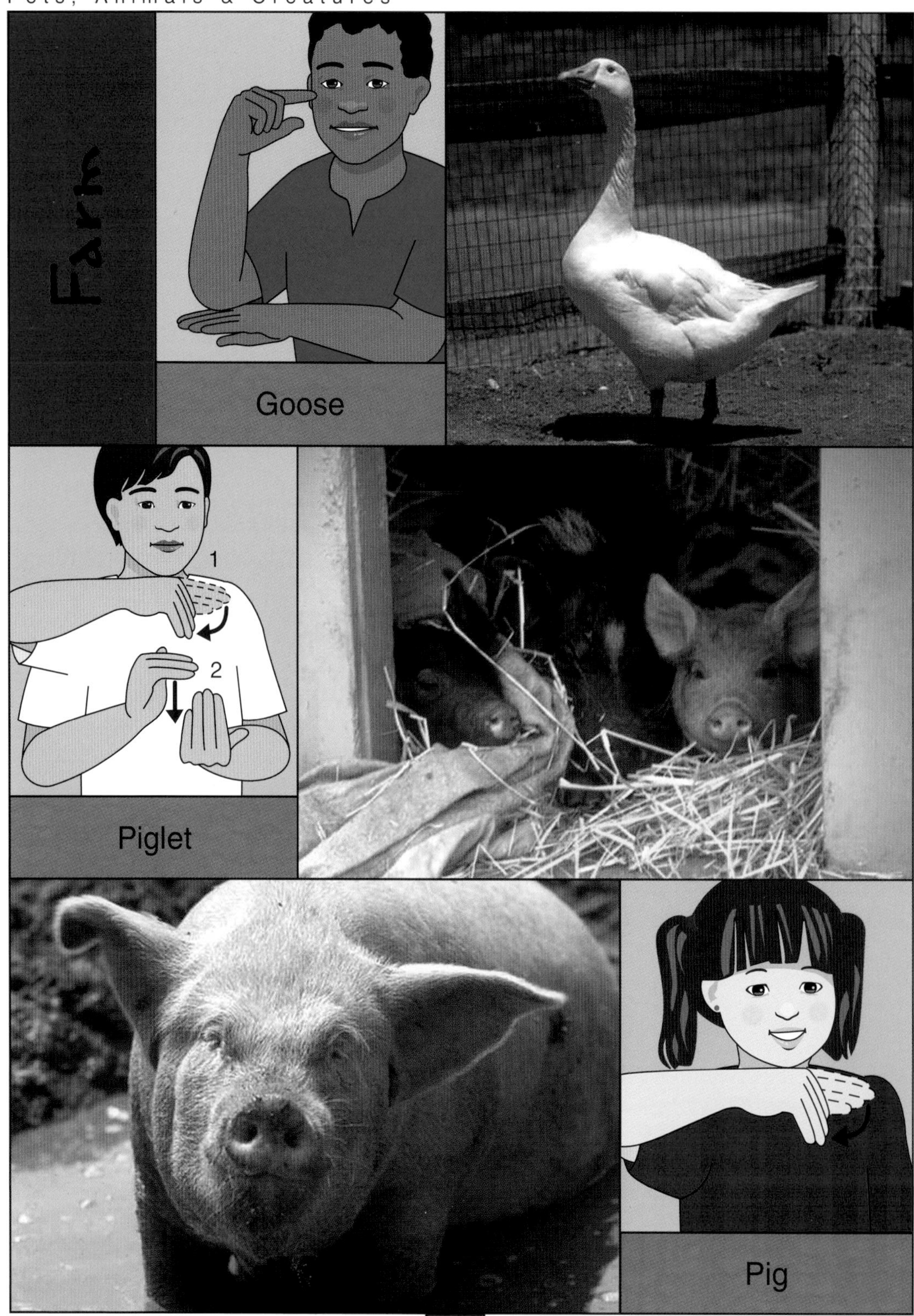
Farm
Goose
1
2
Piglet
Pig

Farm
Cow
Calf
Horse

Farm

Sheep

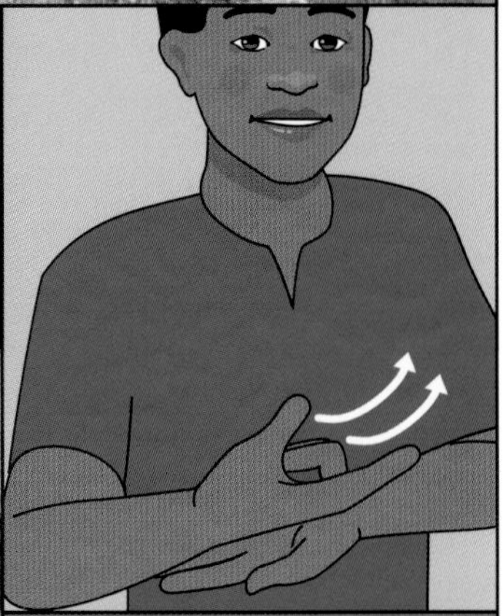

Lamb

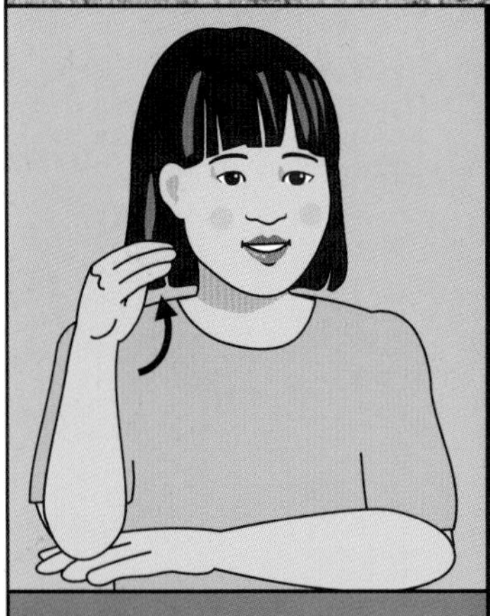

Swan

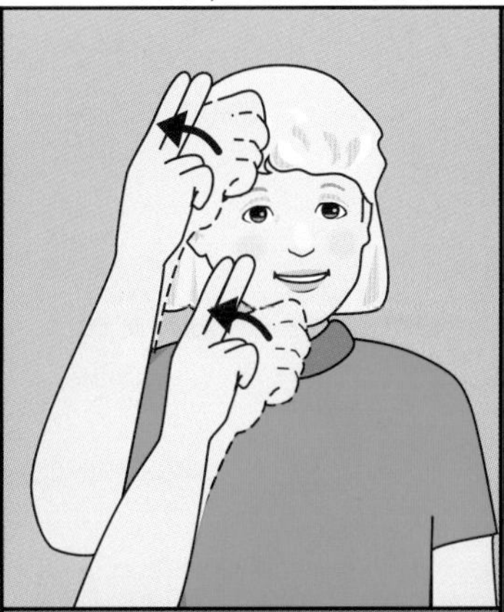

Farm

Goat

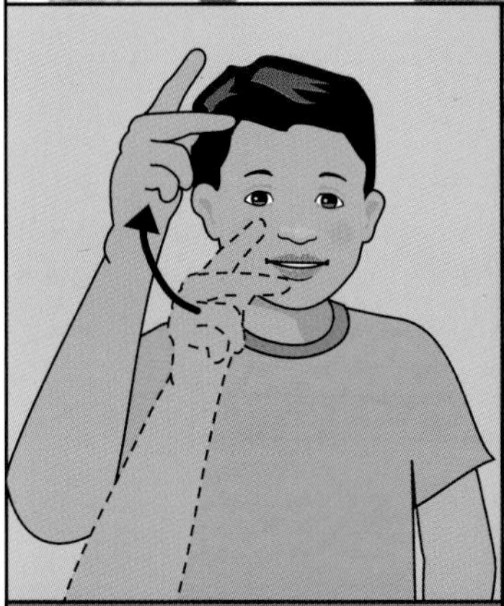

Kid

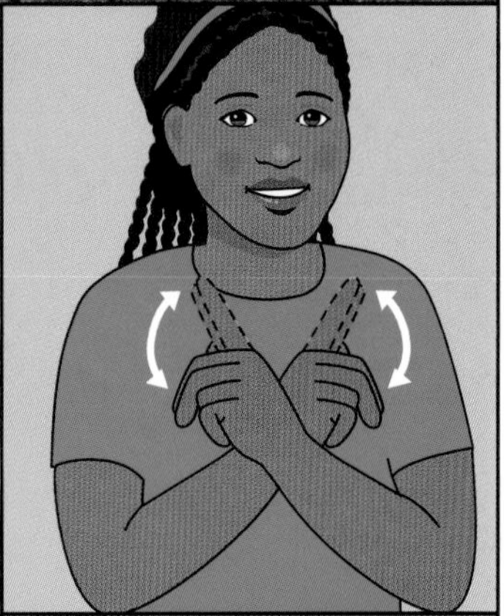

Rabbit

Chicken

Rooster

Turkey

Farm
Donkey
Duck
Duckling

Forest
Raccoon
Deer
Wolf

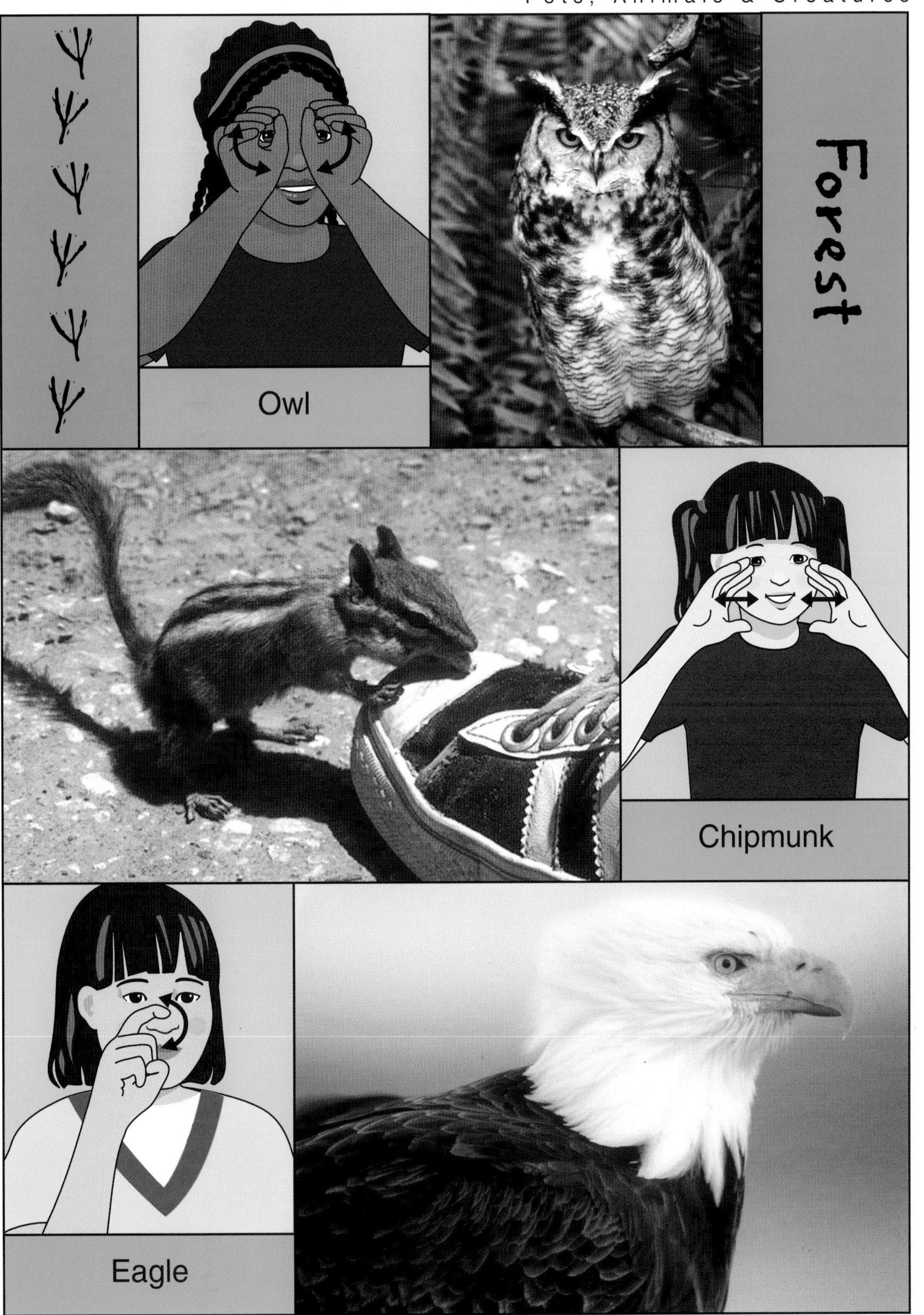
Forest
Owl
Chipmunk
Eagle

Forest

Bear

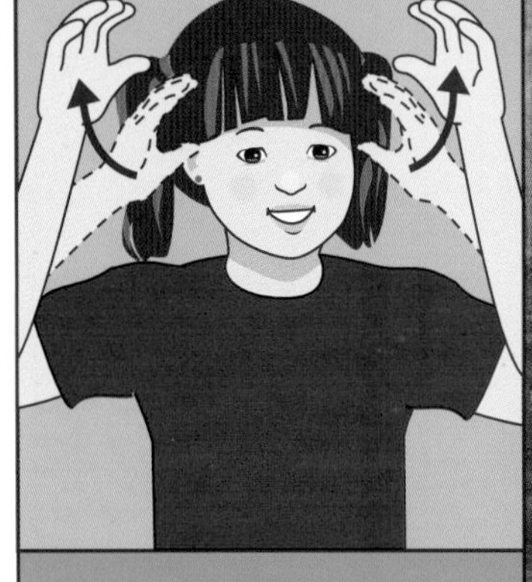

Moose

Forest
Panda
Squirrel
Porcupine

Elk

Gorilla

Fox

Polar
Penguin
Reindeer
Polar Bear

Grassland

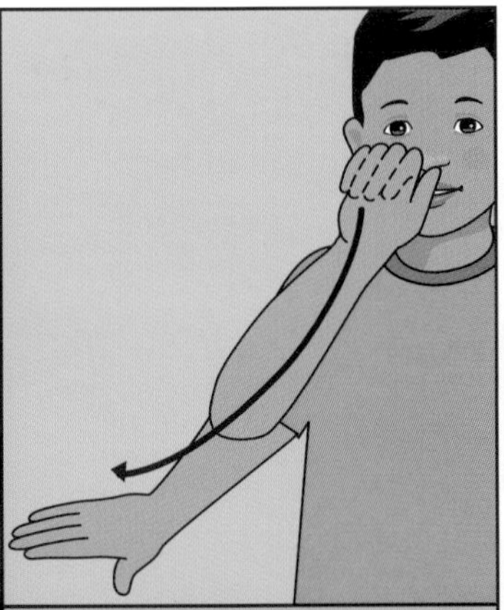

Elephant

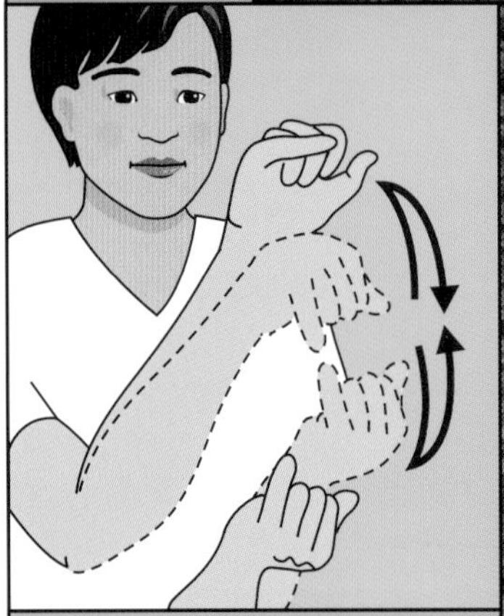

Hippo

Leopard

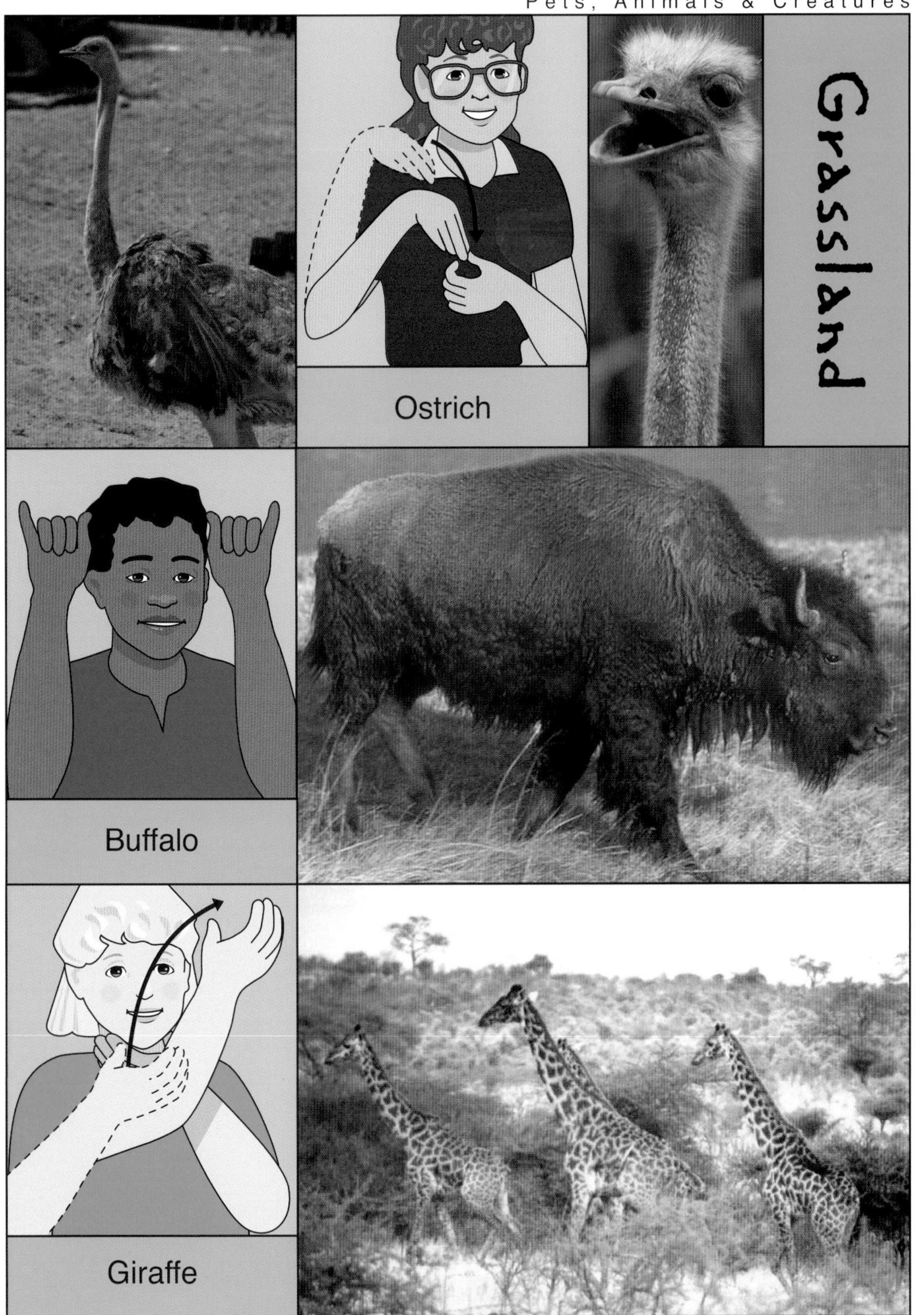
Grassland
Ostrich
Buffalo
Giraffe

Grassland
Rhinoceros
Peacock
Monkey

Grassland
Tiger
Lion
1
2
Zebra

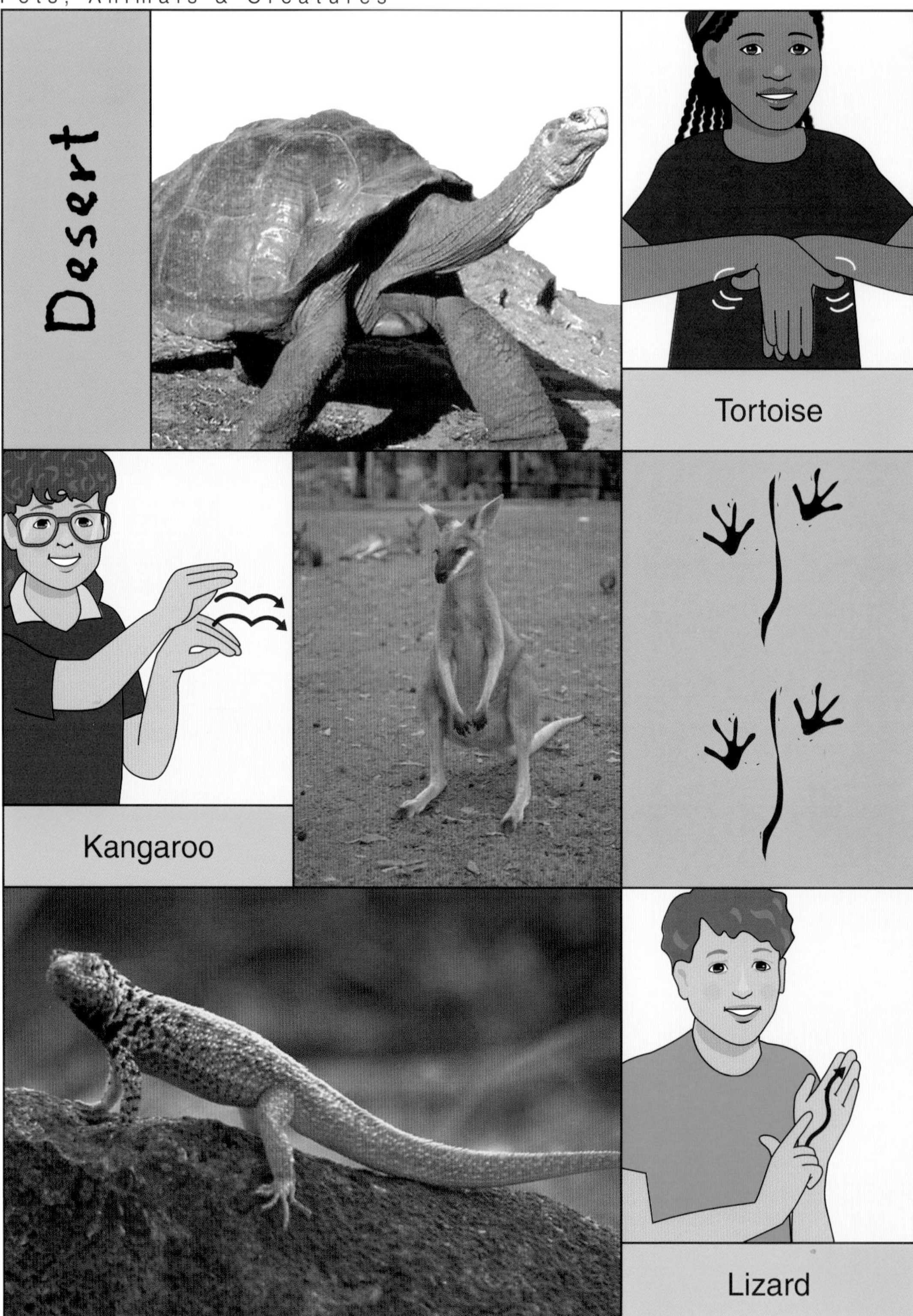
Desert
Tortoise
Kangaroo
Lizard

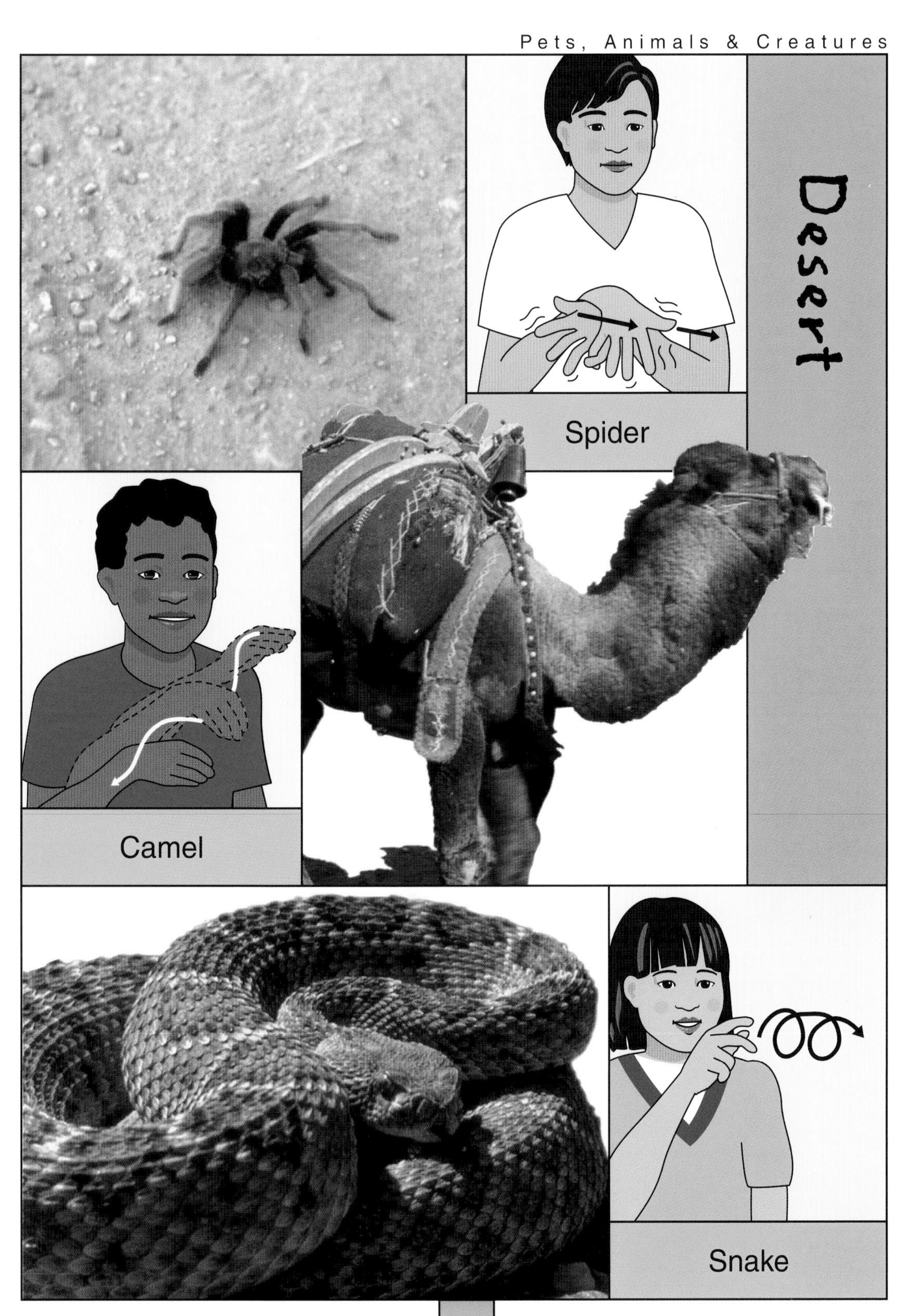
Desert
Spider
Camel
Snake

Water

Gull

Seal

Crocodile

Water
Whale
Frog
Alligator

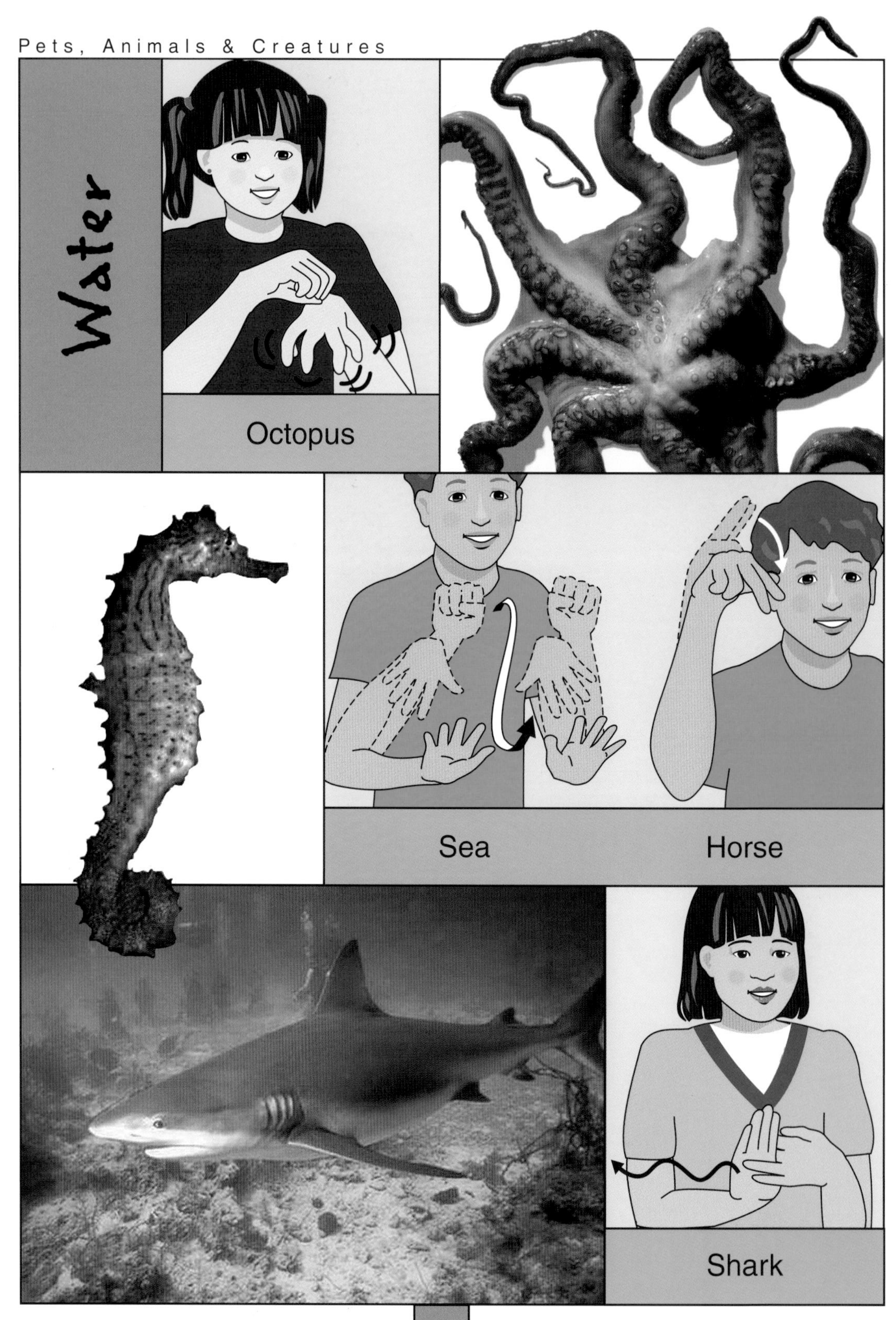
Water
Octopus
Sea
Horse
Shark

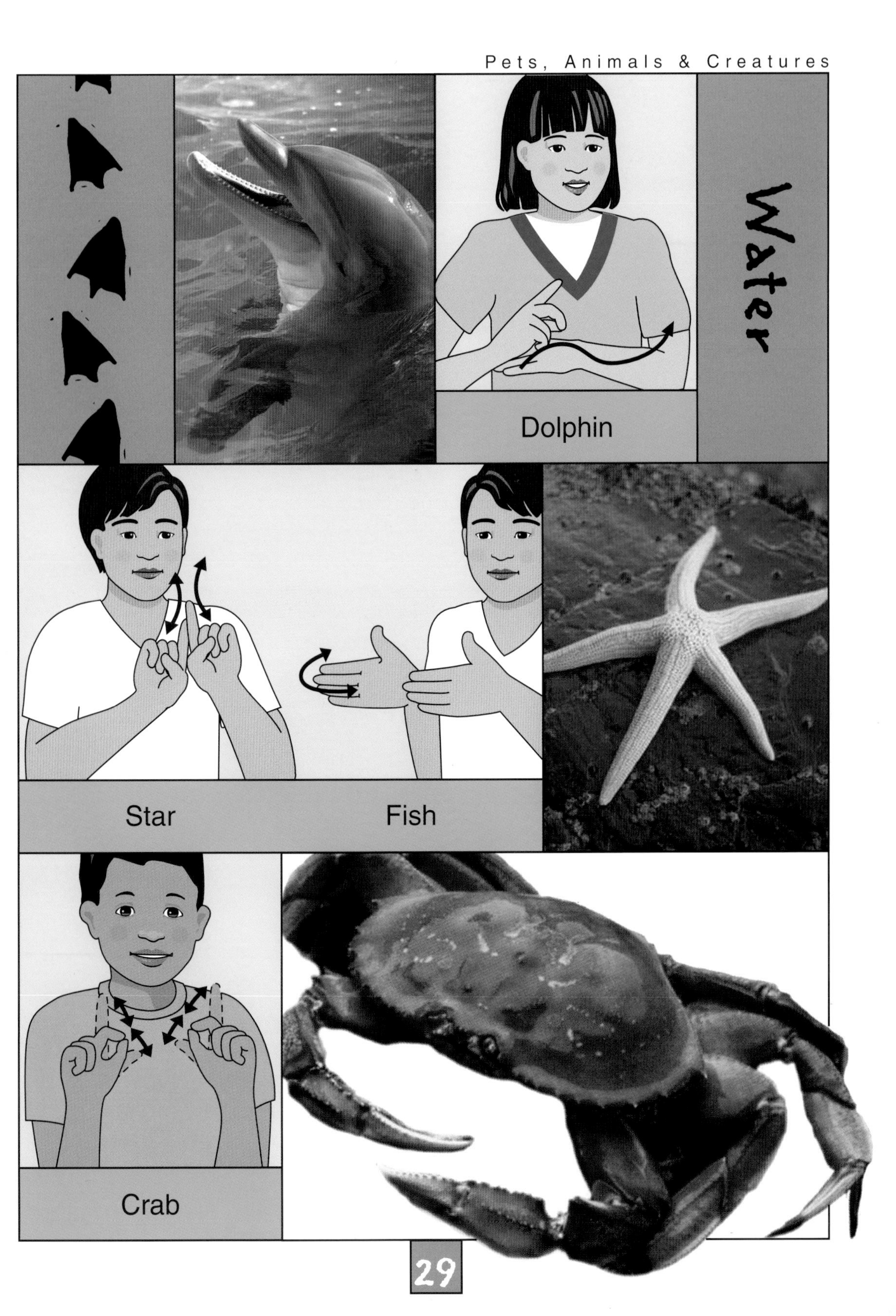
Water
Dolphin
Star
Fish
Crab

Index

Also from Garlic Press

Finger Alphabet GP-046
Uses word games and activities to teach the finger alphabet.

Signing at School GP-047
Presents signs needed in a school setting.

Can I Help? Helping the Hearing Impaired in Emergency Situations
GP-057 Signs, sentences and information to help communicate with the hearing impaired.

Caring for Young Children: Signing for Day Care Providers and Sitters
GP-058 Signs for feelings, directions, activities and foods, bedtime, discipline and comfort-giving.

An Alphabet of Animal Signs
GP-065 Animal illustrations and associated signs for each letter of the alphabet.

Mother Goose in Sign
GP-066 Fully illustrated nursery rhymes.

Number and Letter Games
GP-072 Presents a variety of games involving the finger alphabet and sign numbers.

Expanded Songs in Sign
GP-005 Eleven songs in Signed English. The easy-to-follow illustrations enable you to sign along.

Foods GP-087
A colorful collection of photos with signs for 43 common foods.

Fruits & Vegetables GP-088
Thirty-nine beautiful photos with signs.

Pets, Animals & Creatures
GP-089 Seventy-seven photos with signs of pets, animals & creatures familiar to signers of all ages.

Signing at Church
GP-098 For adults and young adults. Helpful phrases, the Lord's Prayer and *John 3:16*.

Signing at Sunday School
GP-099 Phrases, songs, Bible verses and the story of Jesus clearly illustrated.

Family and Community
GP-073 Signs for relationships and family and community members in their job roles.

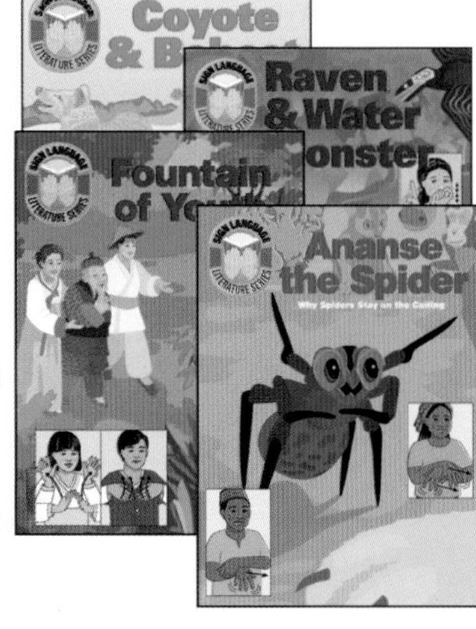

Coyote & Bobcat
GP-081 A Navajo story serving to tell how Coyote and Bobcat got their shapes.

Raven & Water Monster
GP-082 This Haida story tells how Raven gained his beautiful black color and how he brought water to the earth.

Fountain of Youth
GP-086 This Korean folk tale about neighbors shows the rewards of kindness and the folly of greed.

Ananse the Spider: Why Spiders Stay on the Ceiling
GP-085 A West African folk tale about the boastful spider Ananse and why he now hides in dark corners.

www.garlicpress.com